Dear God,

To begin your Journey in your relationship with God whether you are already saved or just need to rededicate your life, your heart and your soul You can pray something like this:

"God, thank You for loving me. I believe that Your Son, Jesus, died to pay for my sins because of Your great love for me. I believe you raised Jesus from the dead. I now put my trust only in Jesus to love me and forgive me for my sins. Help me put Jesus first. Thank you for our new relationship and the gift of eternal life. Amen."

This Journal is for you to write your letters to God, to share your thoughts, feelings and opinions as you grow your faith and strengthen your relationship with God for the rest of the days of your life. It is to express love, anger and all of the rainbows of emotions for God wants and loves everything that makes up the magnificent person you are.

~Lisa Christiansen

Dear God,

To live in gratitude one must live in forgiveness, forgiveness will set you free.

Dear God,

To live in gratitude one must live in forgiveness, forgiveness will set you free.

Dear God,

To live in gratitude one must live in forgiveness, forgiveness will set you free.

Dear God,

To live in gratitude one must live in forgiveness, forgiveness will set you free.

Dear God,

To live in gratitude one must live in forgiveness, forgiveness will set you free.

Dear God,

To live in gratitude one must live in forgiveness, forgiveness will set you free.

Dear God,

To live in gratitude one must live in forgiveness, forgiveness will set you free.

Dear God,

To live in gratitude one must live in forgiveness, forgiveness will set you free.

Dear God,

To live in gratitude one must live in forgiveness, forgiveness will set you free.

Dear God,

To live in gratitude one must live in forgiveness, forgiveness will set you free.

Dear God,

To live in gratitude one must live in forgiveness, forgiveness will set you free.

Dear God,

To live in gratitude one must live in forgiveness, forgiveness will set you free.

Dear God,

Dear God,

To live in gratitude one must live in forgiveness, forgiveness will set you free.

Dear God,

To live in gratitude one must live in forgiveness, forgiveness will set you free.

Dear God,

To live in gratitude one must live in forgiveness, forgiveness will set you free.

Dear God,

To live in gratitude one must live in forgiveness, forgiveness will set you free.

Dear God,

To live in gratitude one must live in forgiveness, forgiveness will set you free.

Dear God,

Dear God,

To live in gratitude one must live in forgiveness, forgiveness will set you free.

Dear God,

To live in gratitude one must live in forgiveness, forgiveness will set you free.

Dear God,

To live in gratitude one must live in forgiveness, forgiveness will set you free.

Dear God,

To live in gratitude one must live in forgiveness, forgiveness will set you free.

Dear God,

To live in gratitude one must live in forgiveness, forgiveness will set you free.

Dear God,

To live in gratitude one must live in forgiveness, forgiveness will set you free.

Dear God,

To live in gratitude one must live in forgiveness, forgiveness will set you free.

Dear God,

Dear God,

To live in gratitude one must live in forgiveness, forgiveness will set you free.

Dear God,

Dear God,

Dear God,

Dear God,

To live in gratitude one must live in forgiveness, forgiveness will set you free.

Dear God,

To live in gratitude one must live in forgiveness, forgiveness will set you free.

Dear God,

To live in gratitude one must live in forgiveness, forgiveness will set you free.

Dear God,

To live in gratitude one must live in forgiveness, forgiveness will set you free.

Dear God,

To live in gratitude one must live in forgiveness, forgiveness will set you free.

Dear God,

To live in gratitude one must live in forgiveness, forgiveness will set you free.

Dear God,

Dear God,

To live in gratitude one must live in forgiveness, forgiveness will set you free.

Dear God,

Dear God,

To live in gratitude one must live in forgiveness, forgiveness will set you free.

Dear God,

To live in gratitude one must live in forgiveness, forgiveness will set you free.

Dear God,

To live in gratitude one must live in forgiveness, forgiveness will set you free.

Dear God,

To live in gratitude one must live in forgiveness, forgiveness will set you free.

Dear God,

To live in gratitude one must live in forgiveness, forgiveness will set you free.

Dear God,

To live in gratitude one must live in forgiveness, forgiveness will set you free.

Dear God,

To live in gratitude one must live in forgiveness, forgiveness will set you free.

Dear God,

To live in gratitude one must live in forgiveness, forgiveness will set you free.

Dear God,

To live in gratitude one must live in forgiveness, forgiveness will set you free.

Dear God,

To live in gratitude one must live in forgiveness, forgiveness will set you free.

Dear God,

To live in gratitude one must live in forgiveness, forgiveness will set you free.

Dear God,

To live in gratitude one must live in forgiveness, forgiveness will set you free.

Dear God,

To live in gratitude one must live in forgiveness, forgiveness will set you free.

Dear God,

To live in gratitude one must live in forgiveness, forgiveness will set you free.

Dear God,

To live in gratitude one must live in forgiveness, forgiveness will set you free.

Dear God,

To live in gratitude one must live in forgiveness, forgiveness will set you free.

Dear God,

To live in gratitude one must live in forgiveness, forgiveness will set you free.

Dear God,

To live in gratitude one must live in forgiveness, forgiveness will set you free.

Dear God,

To live in gratitude one must live in forgiveness, forgiveness will set you free.

Dear God,

To live in gratitude one must live in forgiveness, forgiveness will set you free.

Dear God,

To live in gratitude one must live in forgiveness, forgiveness will set you free.

Dear God,

To live in gratitude one must live in forgiveness, forgiveness will set you free.

Dear God,

To live in gratitude one must live in forgiveness, forgiveness will set you free.

Dear God,

To live in gratitude one must live in forgiveness, forgiveness will set you free.

Dear God,

To live in gratitude one must live in forgiveness, forgiveness will set you free.

Dear God,

Dear God,

To live in gratitude one must live in forgiveness, forgiveness will set you free.

Dear God,

Dear God,

To live in gratitude one must live in forgiveness, forgiveness will set you free.

Dear God,

To live in gratitude one must live in forgiveness, forgiveness will set you free.

Dear God,

To live in gratitude one must live in forgiveness, forgiveness will set you free.

Dear God,

To live in gratitude one must live in forgiveness, forgiveness will set you free.

Dear God,

To live in gratitude one must live in forgiveness, forgiveness will set you free.

Dear God,

To live in gratitude one must live in forgiveness, forgiveness will set you free.

Dear God,

To live in gratitude one must live in forgiveness, forgiveness will set you free.

Dear God,

To live in gratitude one must live in forgiveness, forgiveness will set you free.

Dear God,

To live in gratitude one must live in forgiveness, forgiveness will set you free.

Dear God,

To live in gratitude one must live in forgiveness, forgiveness will set you free.

Dear God,

To live in gratitude one must live in forgiveness, forgiveness will set you free.

Dear God,

Dear God,

To live in gratitude one must live in forgiveness, forgiveness will set you free.

Dear God,

To live in gratitude one must live in forgiveness, forgiveness will set you free.

Dear God,

To live in gratitude one must live in forgiveness, forgiveness will set you free.

Dear God,

To live in gratitude one must live in forgiveness, forgiveness will set you free.

Dear God,

To live in gratitude one must live in forgiveness, forgiveness will set you free.

Dear God,

To live in gratitude one must live in forgiveness, forgiveness will set you free.

Dear God,

To live in gratitude one must live in forgiveness, forgiveness will set you free.

Dear God,

To live in gratitude one must live in forgiveness, forgiveness will set you free.

Dear God,

To live in gratitude one must live in forgiveness, forgiveness will set you free.

Dear God,

To live in gratitude one must live in forgiveness, forgiveness will set you free.

Dear God,

To live in gratitude one must live in forgiveness, forgiveness will set you free.

Dear God,

To live in gratitude one must live in forgiveness, forgiveness will set you free.

Dear God,

To live in gratitude one must live in forgiveness, forgiveness will set you free.

Dear God,

To live in gratitude one must live in forgiveness, forgiveness will set you free.

Dear God,

To live in gratitude one must live in forgiveness, forgiveness will set you free.

Dear God,

To live in gratitude one must live in forgiveness, forgiveness will set you free.

Dear God,

Dear God,

To live in gratitude one must live in forgiveness, forgiveness will set you free.

Dear God,

Dear God,

To live in gratitude one must live in forgiveness, forgiveness will set you free.

Dear God,

To live in gratitude one must live in forgiveness, forgiveness will set you free.

Dear God,

Dear God,

To live in gratitude one must live in forgiveness, forgiveness will set you free.

Dear God,

To live in gratitude one must live in forgiveness, forgiveness will set you free.

Dear God,

To live in gratitude one must live in forgiveness, forgiveness will set you free.

Dear God,

To live in gratitude one must live in forgiveness, forgiveness will set you free.

Dear God,

To live in gratitude one must live in forgiveness, forgiveness will set you free.

Dear God,

To live in gratitude one must live in forgiveness, forgiveness will set you free.

Dear God,

To live in gratitude one must live in forgiveness, forgiveness will set you free.

Dear God,

To live in gratitude one must live in forgiveness, forgiveness will set you free.

Dear God,

To live in gratitude one must live in forgiveness, forgiveness will set you free.

Dear God,

Dear God,

Dear God,

To live in gratitude one must live in forgiveness, forgiveness will set you free.

Dear God,

Dear God,

To live in gratitude one must live in forgiveness, forgiveness will set you free.

Dear God,

To live in gratitude one must live in forgiveness, forgiveness will set you free.

Dear God,

To live in gratitude one must live in forgiveness, forgiveness will set you free.

Dear God,

To live in gratitude one must live in forgiveness, forgiveness will set you free.

Dear God,

To live in gratitude one must live in forgiveness, forgiveness will set you free.

Dear God,

Dear God,

To live in gratitude one must live in forgiveness, forgiveness will set you free.

Dear God,

To live in gratitude one must live in forgiveness, forgiveness will set you free.

Dear God,

Dear God,

To live in gratitude one must live in forgiveness, forgiveness will set you free.

Dear God,

Dear God,

Dear God,

Dear God,

To live in gratitude one must live in forgiveness, forgiveness will set you free.

Dear God,

To live in gratitude one must live in forgiveness, forgiveness will set you free.

Dear God,

To live in gratitude one must live in forgiveness, forgiveness will set you free.

Dear God,

Dear God,

To live in gratitude one must live in forgiveness, forgiveness will set you free.

Dear God,

To live in gratitude one must live in forgiveness, forgiveness will set you free.

Dear God,

To live in gratitude one must live in forgiveness, forgiveness will set you free.

Dear God,

To live in gratitude one must live in forgiveness, forgiveness will set you free.

Dear God,

To live in gratitude one must live in forgiveness, forgiveness will set you free.

Dear God,

To live in gratitude one must live in forgiveness, forgiveness will set you free.

Dear God,

To live in gratitude one must live in forgiveness, forgiveness will set you free.

Dear God,

To live in gratitude one must live in forgiveness, forgiveness will set you free.

Dear God,

To live in gratitude one must live in forgiveness, forgiveness will set you free.

Dear God,

To live in gratitude one must live in forgiveness, forgiveness will set you free.

Dear God,

To live in gratitude one must live in forgiveness, forgiveness will set you free.

Dear God,

To live in gratitude one must live in forgiveness, forgiveness will set you free.

Dear God,

To live in gratitude one must live in forgiveness, forgiveness will set you free.

Dear God,

To live in gratitude one must live in forgiveness, forgiveness will set you free.

Dear God,

To live in gratitude one must live in forgiveness, forgiveness will set you free.

Dear God,

To live in gratitude one must live in forgiveness, forgiveness will set you free.

Dear God,

To live in gratitude one must live in forgiveness, forgiveness will set you free.

Dear God,

Dear God,

To live in gratitude one must live in forgiveness, forgiveness will set you free.

Dear God,

To live in gratitude one must live in forgiveness, forgiveness will set you free.

Dear God,

To live in gratitude one must live in forgiveness, forgiveness will set you free.

Dear God,

To live in gratitude one must live in forgiveness, forgiveness will set you free.

Dear God,

Dear God,

To live in gratitude one must live in forgiveness, forgiveness will set you free.

Dear God,

To live in gratitude one must live in forgiveness, forgiveness will set you free.

Dear God,

To live in gratitude one must live in forgiveness, forgiveness will set you free.

Dear God,

To live in gratitude one must live in forgiveness, forgiveness will set you free.

Dear God,

To live in gratitude one must live in forgiveness, forgiveness will set you free.

Dear God,

To live in gratitude one must live in forgiveness, forgiveness will set you free.

Dear God,

Dear God,

Dear God,

Dear God,

To live in gratitude one must live in forgiveness, forgiveness will set you free.

Dear God,

Dear God,

To live in gratitude one must live in forgiveness, forgiveness will set you free.

Dear God,

To live in gratitude one must live in forgiveness, forgiveness will set you free.

Dear God,

To live in gratitude one must live in forgiveness, forgiveness will set you free.

Dear God,

To live in gratitude one must live in forgiveness, forgiveness will set you free.

Dear God,

To live in gratitude one must live in forgiveness, forgiveness will set you free.

Dear God,

To live in gratitude one must live in forgiveness, forgiveness will set you free.

Dear God,

To live in gratitude one must live in forgiveness, forgiveness will set you free.

Dear God,

Dear God,

To live in gratitude one must live in forgiveness, forgiveness will set you free.

Dear God,

To live in gratitude one must live in forgiveness, forgiveness will set you free.

Dear God,

To live in gratitude one must live in forgiveness, forgiveness will set you free.

Dear God,

To live in gratitude one must live in forgiveness, forgiveness will set you free.

Dear God,

To live in gratitude one must live in forgiveness, forgiveness will set you free.

Dear God,

To live in gratitude one must live in forgiveness, forgiveness will set you free.

Dear God,

To live in gratitude one must live in forgiveness, forgiveness will set you free.

Dear God,

To live in gratitude one must live in forgiveness, forgiveness will set you free.

Dear God,

To live in gratitude one must live in forgiveness, forgiveness will set you free.

Dear God,

To live in gratitude one must live in forgiveness, forgiveness will set you free.

Dear God,

To live in gratitude one must live in forgiveness, forgiveness will set you free.

Dear God,

To live in gratitude one must live in forgiveness, forgiveness will set you free.

Dear God,

To live in gratitude one must live in forgiveness, forgiveness will set you free.

Dear God,

To live in gratitude one must live in forgiveness, forgiveness will set you free.

Dear God,

Dear God,

To live in gratitude one must live in forgiveness, forgiveness will set you free.

Dear God,

To live in gratitude one must live in forgiveness, forgiveness will set you free.

Dear God,

To live in gratitude one must live in forgiveness, forgiveness will set you free.

Dear God,

Dear God,

Dear God,

To live in gratitude one must live in forgiveness, forgiveness will set you free.

Dear God,

To live in gratitude one must live in forgiveness, forgiveness will set you free.

Dear God,

To live in gratitude one must live in forgiveness, forgiveness will set you free.

Dear God,

To live in gratitude one must live in forgiveness, forgiveness will set you free.

Dear God,

To live in gratitude one must live in forgiveness, forgiveness will set you free.

Dear God,

To live in gratitude one must live in forgiveness, forgiveness will set you free.

Dear God,

To live in gratitude one must live in forgiveness, forgiveness will set you free.

Dear God,

To live in gratitude one must live in forgiveness, forgiveness will set you free.

Dear God,

Dear God,

To live in gratitude one must live in forgiveness, forgiveness will set you free.

Dear God,

To live in gratitude one must live in forgiveness, forgiveness will set you free.

Dear God,

To live in gratitude one must live in forgiveness, forgiveness will set you free.

Dear God,

To live in gratitude one must live in forgiveness, forgiveness will set you free.

Dear God,

Dear God,

To live in gratitude one must live in forgiveness, forgiveness will set you free.

Dear God,

To live in gratitude one must live in forgiveness, forgiveness will set you free.

Dear God,

To live in gratitude one must live in forgiveness, forgiveness will set you free.

Dear God,

To live in gratitude one must live in forgiveness, forgiveness will set you free.

Dear God,

To live in gratitude one must live in forgiveness, forgiveness will set you free.

Dear God,

To live in gratitude one must live in forgiveness, forgiveness will set you free.

Dear God,

To live in gratitude one must live in forgiveness, forgiveness will set you free.

Dear God,

To live in gratitude one must live in forgiveness, forgiveness will set you free.

Dear God,

To live in gratitude one must live in forgiveness, forgiveness will set you free.

Dear God,

To live in gratitude one must live in forgiveness, forgiveness will set you free.

Dear God,

To live in gratitude one must live in forgiveness, forgiveness will set you free.

Dear God,

To live in gratitude one must live in forgiveness, forgiveness will set you free.

Dear God,

To live in gratitude one must live in forgiveness, forgiveness will set you free.

Dear God,

Dear God,

To live in gratitude one must live in forgiveness, forgiveness will set you free.

Dear God,

To live in gratitude one must live in forgiveness, forgiveness will set you free.

Dear God,

To live in gratitude one must live in forgiveness, forgiveness will set you free.

Dear God,

To live in gratitude one must live in forgiveness, forgiveness will set you free.

Dear God,

To live in gratitude one must live in forgiveness, forgiveness will set you free.

Dear God,

To live in gratitude one must live in forgiveness, forgiveness will set you free.

Dear God,

To live in gratitude one must live in forgiveness, forgiveness will set you free.

Dear God,

Dear God,

To live in gratitude one must live in forgiveness, forgiveness will set you free.

Dear God,

To live in gratitude one must live in forgiveness, forgiveness will set you free.

Dear God,

To live in gratitude one must live in forgiveness, forgiveness will set you free.

Dear God,

To live in gratitude one must live in forgiveness, forgiveness will set you free.

Dear God,

To live in gratitude one must live in forgiveness, forgiveness will set you free.

Dear God,

To live in gratitude one must live in forgiveness, forgiveness will set you free.

Dear God,

Dear God,

To live in gratitude one must live in forgiveness, forgiveness will set you free.

Dear God,

Dear God,

Dear God,

To live in gratitude one must live in forgiveness, forgiveness will set you free.

Dear God,

To live in gratitude one must live in forgiveness, forgiveness will set you free.

Dear God,

To live in gratitude one must live in forgiveness, forgiveness will set you free.

Dear God,

Dear God,

Dear God,

Dear God,

To live in gratitude one must live in forgiveness, forgiveness will set you free.

Dear God,

Dear God,

To live in gratitude one must live in forgiveness, forgiveness will set you free.

Dear God,

To live in gratitude one must live in forgiveness, forgiveness will set you free.

Dear God,

To live in gratitude one must live in forgiveness, forgiveness will set you free.

Dear God,

To live in gratitude one must live in forgiveness, forgiveness will set you free.

Dear God,

Dear God,

To live in gratitude one must live in forgiveness, forgiveness will set you free.

Dear God,

To live in gratitude one must live in forgiveness, forgiveness will set you free.

Dear God,

To live in gratitude one must live in forgiveness, forgiveness will set you free.

Dear God,

To live in gratitude one must live in forgiveness, forgiveness will set you free.

Dear God,

To live in gratitude one must live in forgiveness, forgiveness will set you free.

Dear God,

To live in gratitude one must live in forgiveness, forgiveness will set you free.

Dear God,

To live in gratitude one must live in forgiveness, forgiveness will set you free.

Dear God,

To live in gratitude one must live in forgiveness, forgiveness will set you free.

Dear God,

To live in gratitude one must live in forgiveness, forgiveness will set you free.

Dear God,

To live in gratitude one must live in forgiveness, forgiveness will set you free.

Dear God,

To live in gratitude one must live in forgiveness, forgiveness will set you free.

Dear God,

To live in gratitude one must live in forgiveness, forgiveness will set you free.

Dear God,

Dear God,

To live in gratitude one must live in forgiveness, forgiveness will set you free.

Dear God,

To live in gratitude one must live in forgiveness, forgiveness will set you free.

Dear God,

To live in gratitude one must live in forgiveness, forgiveness will set you free.

www.ingramcontent.com/pod-product-compliance
Lightning Source LLC
Chambersburg PA
CBHW041620020526
44116CB00041B/39